In
1935 if you wanted to
read a good book, you needed
either a lot of money or a library card.
Cheap paperbacks were available, but their
poor production generally mirrored the quality
between the covers. One weekend that year,
Allen Lane, Managing Director of The Bodley Head,
having spent the weekend visiting Agatha Christie,
found himself on a platform at Exeter station trying to
find something to read for his journey back to London.
He was appalled by the quality of the material he had to
choose from. Everything that Allen Lane achieved from that
day until his death in 1970 was based on a passionate belief
in the existence of 'a vast reading public for *intelligent*
books at a low price'. The result of his momentous vision
was the birth not only of Penguin, but of the 'paperback
revolution'. Quality writing became available for the price of
a packet of cigarettes, literature became a mass medium
for the first time, a nation of book-borrowers became a
nation of book-buyers – and the very concept of book
publishing was changed for ever. Those founding
principles – of quality and value, with an overarching
belief in the fundamental importance of reading –
have guided everything the company has
done since 1935. Sir Allen Lane's
pioneering spirit is still very much alive
at Penguin in 2005. Here's to
the next 70 years!

MORE THAN A BUSINESS

'We decided it was time to end the almost customary half-hearted manner in which cheap editions were produced – as though the only people who could possibly want cheap editions must belong to a lower order of intelligence. We, however, believed in the existence in this country of a vast reading public for intelligent books at a low price, and staked everything on it'
Sir Allen Lane, 1902–1970

'The Penguin Books are splendid value for sixpence, so splendid that if other publishers had any sense they would combine against them and suppress them'
George Orwell

'More than a business ... a national cultural asset'
Guardian

'When you look at the whole Penguin achievement you know that it constitutes, in action, one of the more democratic successes of our recent social history'
Richard Hoggart

Cogs in the
Great Machine

ERIC SCHLOSSER

PENGUIN BOOKS

PENGUIN BOOKS

Published by the Penguin Group
Penguin Books Ltd, 80 Strand, London WC2R ORL, England
Penguin Group (USA) Inc., 375 Hudson Street, New York, New York 10014, USA
Penguin Group (Canada), 10 Alcorn Avenue, Toronto, Ontario, Canada M4V 3B2
(a division of Pearson Penguin Canada Inc.)
Penguin Ireland, 25 St Stephen's Green, Dublin 2, Ireland
(a division of Penguin Books Ltd)
Penguin Group (Australia), 250 Camberwell Road, Camberwell, Victoria 3124,
Australia (a division of Pearson Australia Group Pty Ltd)
Penguin Books India Pvt Ltd, 11 Community Centre,
Panchsheel Park, New Delhi – 110 017, India
Penguin Group (NZ), cnr Airborne and Rosedale Roads, Albany,
Auckland 1310, New Zealand (a division of Pearson New Zealand Ltd)
Penguin Books (South Africa) (Pty) Ltd, 24 Sturdee Avenue,
Rosebank 2196, South Africa

Penguin Books Ltd, Registered Offices: 80 Strand, London WC2R ORL, England

www.penguin.com

Fast Food Nation first published 2001
This extract published as a Pocket Penguin 2005

I

Set in 11/13pt Monotype Dante
Typeset by Palimpsest Book Production Limited
Polmont, Stirlingshire
Printed in England by Clays Ltd, St Ives plc

On the Range

Hank was the first person I met in Colorado Springs. He was a prominent local rancher, and I'd called him to learn how development pressures and the dictates of the fast food industry were affecting the area's cattle business. In July of 1997, he offered to give me a tour of the new subdivisions that were rising on land where cattle once roamed. We met in the lobby of my hotel. Hank was forty-two years old and handsome enough to be a Hollywood cowboy, tall and rugged, wearing blue jeans, old boots, and a big white hat. But the Dodge minivan he drove didn't quite go with that image, and he was too smart to fit any stereotype. Hank proved to be good company from the first handshake. He had strong opinions, but didn't take himself too seriously. We spent hours driving around Colorado Springs, looking at how the New West was burying the Old.

As we drove through neighborhoods like Broadmoor Oaks and Broadmoor Bluffs, amid the foothills of Cheyenne Mountain, Hank pointed out that all these big new houses on small lots sat on land that every few generations burned. The houses were surrounded by lovely pale brown grasses, tumbleweed, and scrub oak – ideal kindling. As in southern California, these hillsides could erupt in flames with the slightest spark, a cigarette tossed from a car window. The homes looked solid and prosperous, gave no hint of their vulnerability, and had wonderful views.

Hank's ranch was about twenty miles south of town. As we headed there, the landscape opened up and began to show glimpses of the true West – the wide-open countryside that draws its beauty from the absence of people, attracts people, and then slowly loses its appeal. Through leadership positions in a variety of local and statewide groups, Hank was trying to bridge the gap between ranchers and environmentalists, to establish some common ground between longtime enemies. He was not a wealthy, New Age type playing at being a cowboy. His income came from the roughly four hundred head of cattle on his ranch. He didn't care what was politically correct and had little patience for urban environmentalists who vilified the cattle industry. In his view, good ranchers did far less damage to the land than city-dwellers. 'Nature isn't an abstraction for me,' he said. 'My family lives with it every day.'

When we got to the ranch, Hank's wife, Susan, was leading her horse out of a ring. She was blond and attractive, but no pushover: tall, fit, and strong. Their daughters, Allie and Kris, aged six and eight, ran over to greet us, full of excitement that their dad was home and had brought a visitor. They scrambled into the minivan and joined us for a drive around the property. Hank wanted me to see the difference between his form of ranching and 'raping the land.' As we took off onto a dirt road, I looked back at his house and thought about how small it looked amid this landscape. On acreage hundreds if not thousands of times larger than the front lawns and back yards surrounding the mansions of Colorado Springs, the family lived in a modest log cabin.

Hank was practicing a form of range management inspired by the grazing patterns of elk and buffalo herds, animals who'd lived for millennia on this short-grass prairie. His ranch was divided into thirty-five separate pastures. His cattle spent ten or eleven days in one pasture, then were moved to the next, allowing the native plants, the blue grama and buffalo grass, time to recover. Hank stopped the minivan to show me a nearby stream. On land that has been overgrazed, the stream banks are usually destroyed first, as cattle gather in the cool shade beside the water, eating everything in sight. Hank's stream was fenced off with barbed wire, and the banks were lush and green. Then he took me to see Fountain Creek, which ran straight through the ranch, and I realized that he'd given other guests the same tour. It had a proper sequence and a point.

Fountain Creek was a long, ugly gash about twenty yards wide and fifteen feet deep. The banks were collapsing from erosion, fallen trees and branches littered the creek bed, and a small trickle of water ran down the middle. 'This was done by storm runoff from Colorado Springs,' Hank said. The contrast between his impact on the land and the city's impact was hard to miss. The rapid growth of Colorado Springs had occurred without much official planning, zoning, or spending on drainage projects. As more pavement covered land within the city limits, more water flowed straight into Fountain Creek instead of being absorbed into the ground. The runoff from Colorado Springs eroded the land beside the creek, carrying silt and debris down-stream all the way to Kansas. Hank literally lost part of his ranch every year. It got washed away by the city's rainwater. A nearby rancher once lost ten acres of land in a single day, thanks to runoff from a fierce storm in Colorado Springs. While Hank stood on the crumbling bank, giving an impassioned speech about the water-shed protection group that he'd helped to organize, telling me about holding ponds, landscaped greenways, and the virtues of permeable parking lots covered in gravel, I lost track of his words. And I thought: 'This guy's going to be governor of Colorado someday.'

Toward sunset we spotted a herd of antelope and roared after them. That damn minivan bounced over the prairie like a horse at full gallop, Hank wild behind the wheel, Allie and Kris squealing in the back seat. We had a Chrysler engine, power steering, and disk brakes, but the antelope had a much superior grace, making sharp and unexpected turns, about two dozen of them, bounding effortlessly, butts held high. After a futile chase, Hank let the herd go on its way, then veered right and guided the minivan up a low hill. There was some-thing else he wanted to show me. The girls looked intently out the window, faces flushed, searching for more wildlife. When we reached the crest of the hill, I looked down and saw an immense oval structure, shiny and brand-new. For an instant, I couldn't figure out what it was. It looked like a structure created by some alien civilization and plopped in the middle of nowhere. 'Stock car racing,' Hank said matter-of-factly. The grand-stands around the track were enormous, and so was the parking lot. Acres of black asphalt and white lines now spread across the prairie, thousands of empty spaces waiting for cars.

The speedway was new, and races were being held there every weekend in the summer. You could hear the engines and the crowd from Hank's house. The races weren't the main problem, though. It was the practice runs that bothered Hank and Susan most. In the middle of the day, in one of America's most beautiful landscapes, they would suddenly hear the drone of stock cars going round and round. For a moment, we sat quietly on top of the hill, staring at the speedway bathed in twilight, at this oval strip of pavement, this unsettling omen. Hank stopped there long enough for me to ponder what it meant, the threat now coming his way, then drove back down the hill. The speedway was gone again, out of sight, and the girls were still happy in the back seat, chatting away, oblivious, as the sun dropped behind the mountains.

A New Trust

Ranchers and cowboys have long been the central icons of the American West. Traditionalists have revered them as symbols of freedom and self-reliance. Revisionists have condemned them as racists, economic parasites, and despoilers of the land. The powerful feelings evoked by cattlemen reflect opposing views of our national identity, attempts to sustain old myths or create new ones. There is one indisputable fact, however, about

American ranchers: they are rapidly disappearing. Over the last twenty years, about half a million ranchers sold off their cattle and quit the business. Many of the nation's remaining eight hundred thousand ranchers are faring poorly. They're taking second jobs. They're selling cattle at break-even prices or at a loss. The ranchers who are faring the worst run three to four hundred head of cattle, manage the ranch themselves, and live solely off the proceeds. The sort of hard-working ranchers long idealized in cowboy myths are the ones most likely to go broke today. Without receiving a fraction of the public attention given to the northwestern spotted owl, America's independent cattlemen have truly become an endangered species.

Ranchers currently face a host of economic problems: rising land prices, stagnant beef prices, oversupplies of cattle, increased shipments of live cattle from Canada and Mexico, development pressures, inheritance taxes, health scares about beef. On top of all that, the growth of the fast food chains has encouraged consolidation in the meatpacking industry. McDonald's is the nation's largest purchaser of beef. In 1968, McDonald's bought ground beef from 175 local suppliers. A few years later, seeking to achieve greater product uniformity as it expanded, McDonald's reduced the number of beef suppliers to five. Much like the french fry industry, the meatpacking industry has been transformed by mergers and acquisitions over the last twenty years. Many ranchers now argue that a few large corporations have gained a stranglehold on the market, using unfair tactics to drive down the price of cattle. Anger toward the large meatpackers is growing, and a new range war threatens to erupt, one that will determine the social and economic structure of the rural West.

A century ago, American ranchers found themselves in a similar predicament. The leading sectors of the nation's economy were controlled by corporate alliances known as 'trusts.' There was a Sugar Trust, a Steel Trust, a Tobacco Trust – and a Beef Trust. It set the prices offered for cattle. Ranchers who spoke out against this monopoly power were often blackballed, unable to sell their cattle at any price. In 1917, at the height of the Beef Trust, the five largest meatpacking companies – Armour, Swift, Morris, Wilson, and Cudahy – controlled about 55 percent of the market. The early twentieth century had trusts, but it also had 'trustbusters,' progressive government officials who believed that concentrated economic power posed a grave threat to American democracy. The Sherman Antitrust Act had been passed in 1890 after a congressional investigation of price fixing in the meatpacking industry, and for the next two decades the federal government tried to break up the Beef Trust, with little success. In 1917 President Woodrow Wilson ordered the Federal Trade Commission to investigate the industry. The FTC inquiry concluded that the five major meatpacking firms had secretly fixed prices for years, had colluded to divide up markets, and had shared livestock information to guarantee that ranchers received the lowest possible price for their cattle. Afraid that an antitrust trial might end with an unfavorable verdict, the five meatpacking companies signed a consent decree in 1920 that forced them to sell off their stockyards, retail meat stores, railway interests, and livestock journals. A year later Congress created the Packers and Stockyards Administration (P&SA), a federal agency with a broad authority to prevent price-fixing and monopolistic behavior in the beef industry.

For the next fifty years, ranchers sold their cattle in a relatively competitive marketplace. The price of cattle was set through open bidding at auctions. The large meatpackers competed with hundreds of small regional firms. In 1970 the top four meatpacking firms slaughtered only 21 percent of the nation's cattle. A decade later, the Reagan administration allowed these firms to merge and combine without fear of antitrust enforcement. The Justice Department and the P&SA's successor, the Grain Inspection, Packers and Stockyards Administration (GIPSA), stood aside as the large meatpackers gained control of one local cattle market after another. Today the top four meatpacking firms – ConAgra, IBP, Excel, and National Beef – slaughter about 84 percent of the nation's cattle. Market concentration in the beef industry is now at the highest level since record-keeping began in the early twentieth century.

Today's unprecedented degree of meatpacking concentration has helped depress the prices that independent ranchers get for their cattle. Over the last twenty years, the rancher's share of every retail dollar spent on beef has fallen from 63 cents to 46 cents. The four major meatpacking companies now control about 20 percent of the live cattle in the United States through 'captive supplies' – cattle that are either maintained in company-owned feedlots or purchased in advance through forward contracts. When cattle prices start to rise, the large meatpackers can flood the market with their own captive supplies, driving prices back down. They can also obtain cattle through confidential agreements with wealthy ranchers, never revealing the true price being paid. ConAgra and Excel operate their own gigantic feedlots, while IBP has private arrangements with some of America's biggest ranchers and feeders, including the Bass brothers, Paul Engler, and J. R. Simplot. Independent ranchers and feedlots now have a hard time figuring out what their cattle are actually worth, let alone finding a buyer for them at the right price. On any given day in the nation's regional cattle markets, as much as 80 percent of the cattle being exchanged are captive supplies. The prices being paid for these cattle are never disclosed.

To get a sense of what an independent rancher now faces, imagine how the New York Stock Exchange would function if large investors could keep the terms of all their stock trades secret. Ordinary investors would have no idea what their own stocks were really worth – a fact that wealthy traders could easily exploit. 'A free market requires many buyers as well as many sellers, all with equal access to accurate information, all entitled to trade on the same terms, and none with a big enough share of the market to influence price,' said a report by Nebraska's Center for Rural Affairs. 'Nothing close to these conditions now exists in the cattle market.'

The large meatpacking firms have thus far shown

little interest in buying their own cattle ranches. 'Why would they want the hassle?' Lee Pitts, the editor of *Livestock Market Digest*, told me. 'Raising cattle is a business with a high overhead, and most of the capital's tied up in the land.' Instead of buying their own ranches, the meatpacking companies have been financing a handful of large feedlot owners who lease ranches and run cattle for them. 'It's just another way of controlling prices through captive supply,' Pitts explained. 'The packers now own some of these big feeders lock, stock, and barrel, and tell them exactly what to do.'

The Breasts of Mr. Mcdonald

Many ranchers now fear that the beef industry is deliberately being restructured along the lines of the poultry industry. They do not want to wind up like chicken growers – who in recent years have become virtually powerless, trapped by debt and by onerous contracts written by the large processors. The poultry industry was also transformed by a wave of mergers in the 1980s. Eight chicken processors now control about two-thirds of the American market. These processors have shifted almost all of their production to the rural South, where the weather tends to be mild, the workforce is poor, unions are weak, and farmers are desperate to find some way of staying on their land. Alabama, Arkansas, Georgia, and Mississippi now produce more than half the chicken raised in the United States. Although many factors helped revolutionize the poultry industry and increase the power of the large processors, one innovation played an especially important role. The Chicken McNugget turned a bird that once had to be carved at a table into something that could easily be eaten behind the wheel of a car. It turned a bulk agricultural commodity into a manufactured, value-added product. And it encouraged a system of production that has turned many chicken farmers into little more than serfs.

'I have an idea,' Fred Turner, the chairman of McDonald's, told one of his suppliers in 1979. 'I want a chicken finger-food without bones, about the size of your thumb. Can you do it?' The supplier, an executive at Keystone Foods, ordered a group of technicians to get to work in the lab, where they were soon joined by food scientists from McDonald's. Poultry consumption in the United States was growing, a trend with alarming implications for a fast food chain that only sold hamburgers. The nation's chicken meat had traditionally been provided by hens that were too old to lay eggs; after World War II a new poultry industry based in Delaware and Virginia lowered the cost of raising chicken, while medical research touted the health benefits of eating it. Fred Turner wanted McDonald's to sell a chicken dish that wouldn't clash with the chain's sensibility. After six months of intensive research, the Keystone lab developed new technology for the manufacture of McNuggets – small pieces of reconstituted chicken, composed mainly of white meat, that were held together by stabilizers, breaded, fried, frozen, then reheated. The initial test-marketing of McNuggets was so successful that McDonald's enlisted another company,

Tyson Foods, to guarantee an adequate supply. Based in Arkansas, Tyson was one of the nation's leading chicken processors, and it soon developed a new breed of chicken to facilitate the production of McNuggets. Dubbed 'Mr. McDonald,' the new breed had unusually large breasts.

Chicken McNuggets were introduced nationwide in 1983. Within one month of their launch, the McDonald's Corporation had become the second-largest purchaser of chicken in the United States, surpassed only by KFC. McNuggets tasted good, they were easy to chew, and they appeared to be healthier than other items on the menu at McDonald's. After all, they were made out of chicken. But their health benefits were illusory. A chemical analysis of McNuggets by a researcher at Harvard Medical School found that their 'fatty acid profile' more closely resembled beef than poultry. They were cooked in beef tallow, like McDonald's fries. The chain soon switched to vegetable oil, adding 'beef extract' to McNuggets during the manufacturing process in order to retain their familiar taste. Chicken McNuggets, which became wildly popular among young children, still derive much of their flavor from beef additives – and contain twice as much fat per ounce as a hamburger.

The McNugget helped change not only the American diet but also its system for raising and processing poultry. 'The impact of McNuggets was so huge that it changed the industry,' the president of ConAgra Poultry, the nation's third-largest chicken processor, later acknowledged. Twenty years ago, most chicken was sold whole; today about 90 percent of the chicken sold in the United

States has been cut into pieces, cutlets, or nuggets. In 1992 American consumption of chicken for the first time surpassed the consumption of beef. Gaining the McNugget contract helped turn Tyson Foods into the world's largest chicken processor. Tyson now manufactures about half of the nation's McNuggets and sells chicken to ninety of the one hundred largest restaurant chains. It is a vertically integrated company that breeds, slaughters, and processes chicken. It does not, however, raise the birds. It leaves the capital expenditures and the financial risks of that task to thousands of 'independent contractors.'

A Tyson chicken grower never owns the birds in his or her poultry houses. Like most of the other leading processors, Tyson supplies its growers with one-day-old chicks. Between the day they are born and the day they are killed, the birds spend their entire lives on the grower's property. But they belong to Tyson. The company supplies the feed, veterinary services, and technical support. It determines feeding schedules, demands equipment upgrades, and employs 'flock supervisors' to make sure that corporate directives are being followed. It hires the trucks that drop off the baby chicks and return seven weeks later to pick up full-grown chickens ready for slaughter. At the processing plant, Tyson employees count and weigh the birds. A grower's income is determined by a formula based upon that count, that weight, and the amount of feed used.

The chicken grower provides the land, the labor, the poultry houses, and the fuel. Most growers must borrow money to build the houses, which cost about $150,000 each and hold about 25,000 birds. A 1995 survey by Louisiana Tech University found that the typical grower had been raising chicken for fifteen years, owned three poultry houses, remained deeply in debt, and earned perhaps $12,000 a year. About half of the nation's chicken growers leave the business after just three years, either selling out or losing everything. The back roads of rural Arkansas are now littered with abandoned poultry houses.

Most chicken growers cannot obtain a bank loan without already having a signed contract from a major processor. 'We get the check first,' a loan officer told the *Arkansas Democrat-Gazette*. A chicken grower who is unhappy with his or her processor has little power to do anything about it. Poultry contracts are short-term. Growers who complain may soon find themselves with empty poultry houses and debts that still need to be paid. Twenty-five years ago, when the United States had dozens of poultry firms, a grower stood a much better chance of finding a new processor and of striking a better deal. Today growers who are labeled 'difficult' often have no choice but to find a new line of work. A processor can terminate a contract with a grower whenever it likes. It owns the birds. Short of that punishment, a processor can prolong the interval between the departure of one flock and the arrival of another. Every day that poultry houses sit empty, the grower loses money.

The large processors won't publicly disclose the terms of their contracts. In the past, such contracts have not only required that growers surrender all rights to file a lawsuit against the company, but have also forbidden them from joining any association that might link growers in a strong bargaining unit. The processors do not like the idea of chicken growers joining forces to protect their interests. 'Our relationship with our growers is a one-on-one contractual relationship . . .' a Tyson executive told a reporter in 1998. 'We want to see that it remains that way.'

Captives

The four large meatpacking firms claim that an oversupply of beef, not any corporate behavior, is responsible for the low prices that American ranchers are paid for their cattle. A number of studies by the U.S. Department of Agriculture (USDA) have reached the same conclusion. Annual beef consumption in the United States peaked in 1976, at about ninety-four pounds per person. Today the typical American eats about sixty-eight pounds of beef every year. Although the nation's population has grown since the 1970s, it has not grown fast enough to compensate for the decline in beef consumption. Ranchers trying to stabilize their incomes fell victim to their own fallacy of composition. They followed the advice of agribusiness firms and gave their cattle growth hormones. As a result, cattle are much bigger today; fewer cattle are sold; and most American beef cannot be exported to the European Union, where the use of bovine growth hormones has been banned.

The meatpacking companies claim that captive supplies and formula pricing systems are means of achieving greater efficiency, not of controlling cattle prices. Their slaughterhouses require a large and steady volume of cattle to operate profitably; captive supplies are one reliable way of sustaining that volume. The large meatpacking companies say that they've become a convenient scapegoat for ranchers, when the real problem is low poultry prices. A pound of chicken costs about half as much as a pound of beef. The long-term deals now being offered to cattlemen are portrayed as innovations that will save, not destroy, the beef industry. Responding in 1998 to a USDA investigation of captive supplies in Kansas, IBP defended such 'alternative methods for selling fed cattle.' The company argued that these practices were 'similar to changes that have already occurred . . . for selling other agricultural commodities,' such as poultry.

Many independent ranchers are convinced that captive supplies are used primarily to control the market, not to achieve greater slaughterhouse efficiency. They do not oppose large-scale transactions or long-term contracts; they oppose cattle prices that are kept secret. Most of all, they do not trust the meatpacking giants. The belief that agribusiness executives secretly talk on the phone with their competitors, set prices, and divide up the worldwide market for commodities – a belief widely held among independent ranchers and farmers – may seem like a paranoid fantasy. But that is precisely what executives at Archer Daniels Midland, 'supermarket to the world,' did for years.

Three of Archer Daniels Midland's top officials, including Michael Andreas, its vice chairman, were sent to federal prison in 1999 for conspiring with foreign rivals to control the international market for lysine (an important feed additive). The Justice Department's investigation of this massive price-fixing scheme focused on the period between August of 1992 and December of 1995. Within that roughly three-and-a-half-year stretch, Archer Daniels Midland and its co-conspirators may have overcharged farmers by as much as $180 million. During the same period, Archer Daniels Midland executives also met with their overseas rivals to set the worldwide price for citric acid (a common food additive). At a meeting with Japanese executives that was secretly recorded, the president of Archer Daniels Midland preached the virtues of collaboration. 'We have a saying at this company,' he said. 'Our competitors are our friends, and our customers are our enemies.' Archer Daniels Midland remains the world's largest producer of lysine, as well as the world's largest processor of soybeans and corn. It is also one of the largest shareholders of IBP.

A 1996 USDA investigation of concentration in the beef industry found that many ranchers were afraid to testify against the large meatpacking companies, fearing retaliation and 'economic ruin.' That year Mike Callicrate, a cattleman from St. Francis, Kansas, decided to speak out against corporate behavior he thought was not just improper but criminal. 'I was driving down the road one day,' Callicrate told me, 'and I kept thinking, when is someone going to do something about this?

And I suddenly realized that maybe nobody's going to do it, and I had to give it a try.' He claims that after his testimony before the USDA committee, the large meat-packers promptly stopped bidding on his cattle. 'I couldn't sell my cattle,' he said. 'They'd drive right past my feed yard and buy cattle from a guy two hundred miles further away.' His business has recovered some-what; ConAgra and Excel now bid on his cattle. The experience has turned him into an activist. He refuses to 'make the transition to slavery quietly.' He has spoken at congressional hearings and has joined a dozen other cattlemen in a class-action lawsuit against IBP. The lawsuit claims that IBP has for many years violated the Packers and Stockyards Act through a wide variety of anticompetitive tactics. According to Callicrate, the suit will demonstrate that the company's purported effi-ciency in production is really 'an efficiency in stealing.' IBP denies the charges. 'It makes no sense for us to do anything to hurt cattle producers,' a top IBP executive told a reporter, 'when we depend upon them to supply our plants.'

The Threat of Wealthy Neighbors

The Colorado Cattlemen's Association filed an amicus brief in Mike Callicrate's lawsuit against IBP, demanding a competitive marketplace for cattle and a halt to any ille-gal buying practices being used by the large meatpacking firms. Ranchers in Colorado today, however, face threats to their livelihood that are unrelated to fluctuations in

cattle prices. During the past twenty years, Colorado
has lost roughly 1.5 million acres of ranchland to development. Population growth and the booming market
for vacation homes have greatly driven up land costs.
Some ranchland that sold for less than $200 an acre in
the 1960s now sells for hundreds of times that amount.
The new land prices make it impossible for ordinary
ranchers to expand their operations. Each head of cattle
needs about thirty acres of pasture for grazing, and until
cattle start producing solid gold nuggets instead of
sirloin, it's hard to sustain beef production on such
expensive land. Ranching families in Colorado tend to
be land-rich and cash-poor. Inheritance taxes can claim
more than half of a cattle ranch's land value. Even if a
family manages to operate its ranch profitably, handing
it down to the next generation may require selling off
large chunks of land, thereby diminishing its productive
capacity.

Along with the ranches, Colorado is quickly losing
its ranching culture. Among the students at Harrison
High you see a variety of fashion statements: gangsta
wannabes, skaters, stoners, goths, and punks. What you
don't see – in the shadow of Pikes Peak, in the heart of
the Rocky Mountain West – is anyone dressed even
remotely like a cowboy. Nobody's wearing shirts with
snaps or Justin boots. In 1959, eight of the nation's top
ten TV shows were Westerns. The networks ran thirty-
five Westerns in prime time every week, and places like
Colorado, where real cowboys lived, were the stuff of
youthful daydreams. That America now seems as dead
and distant as the England of King Arthur. I saw

hundreds of high school students in Colorado Springs, and only one of them wore a cowboy hat. His name was Philly Favorite, he played guitar in a band called the Deadites, and his cowboy hat was made out of fake zebra fur.

The median age of Colorado's ranchers and farmers is about fifty-five, and roughly half of the state's open land will change hands during the next two decades – a potential boon for real estate developers. A number of Colorado land trusts are now working to help ranchers obtain conservation easements. In return for donating future development rights to one of these trusts, a rancher receives an immediate tax break and the prospect of lower inheritance taxes. The land remains private property, but by law can never be turned into golf courses, shopping malls, or subdivisions. In 1995 the Colorado Cattlemen's Association formed the first land trust in the United States that is devoted solely to the preservation of ranchland. It has thus far protected almost 40,000 acres, a significant achievement. But ranchland in Colorado is now vanishing at the rate of about 90,000 acres a year.

Conservation easements are usually of greatest benefit to wealthy gentleman ranchers who earn large incomes from other sources. The doctors, lawyers, and stockbrokers now running cattle on some of Colorado's most beautiful land can own big ranches, preserve open space with easements, and enjoy the big tax deductions. Ranchers whose annual income comes entirely from selling cattle usually don't earn enough to benefit from that sort of tax break. And the value of their land, along with the pressure to sell it, often increases when a wealthy neighbor obtains a conservation easement, since the views in the area are more likely to remain unspoiled.

The Colorado ranchers who now face the greatest economic difficulty are the ones who run a few hundred head of cattle, who work their own land, who don't have any outside income, and who don't stand to gain anything from a big tax write-off. They have to compete with gentleman ranchers whose operations don't have to earn a profit and with part-time ranchers whose operations are kept afloat by second jobs. Indeed, the ranchers most likely to be in financial trouble today are the ones who live the life and embody the values supposedly at the heart of the American West. They are independent and self-sufficient, cherish their freedom, believe in hard work – and as a result are now paying the price.

A Broken Link

Hank died in 1998. He took his own life the week before Christmas. He was forty-three.

When I heard the news, it made no sense to me, none at all. The man that I knew was full of fire and ready to go, the kind of person who seemed always to be throwing himself into the middle of things. He did not hide away. He got involved in the community, served on countless boards and committees. He had a fine sense of humor. He loved his family. The way he died seemed to contradict everything else about his life.

It would be wrong to say that Hank's death was caused by the consolidating and homogenizing influence of the fast food chains, by monopoly power in the meatpacking industry, by depressed prices in the cattle market, by the economic forces bankrupting independent ranchers, by the tax laws that favor wealthy ranchers, by the unrelenting push of Colorado's real estate developers. But it would not be entirely wrong. Hank was under enormous pressure at the time of his death. He was trying to find a way of gaining conservation easements that would protect his land but not sacrifice the financial security of his family. Cattle prices had fallen to their lowest point in more than a decade. And El Paso County was planning to build a new highway right through the heart of his ranch. The stress of these things and others led to sleepless nights, then to a depression that spiraled downward fast, and before long he was gone.

The suicide rate among ranchers and farmers in the United States is now about three times higher than the national average. The issue briefly received attention during the 1980s farm crisis, but has been pretty much ignored ever since. Meanwhile, across rural America, a slow and steady death toll mounts. As the rancher's traditional way of life is destroyed, so are many of the beliefs that go with it. The code of the rancher could hardly be more out of step with America's current state of mind. In Silicon Valley, entrepreneurs and venture capitalists regard failure as just a first step toward success. After three failed Internet start-ups, there's still a chance that the fourth one will succeed. What's being sold ultimately matters less than how well it sells. In ranching, a failure is much more likely to be final. The land that has been lost is not just a commodity. It has meaning that cannot be measured in dollars and cents. It is a tangible connection with the past, something that was meant to be handed down to children and never sold. As Osha Gray Davidson observes in his book *Broken Heartland* (1996), 'To fail several generations of relatives . . . to see yourself as the one weak link in a strong chain . . . is a terrible, and for some, an unbearable burden.'

When Hank was eight years old, he was the subject of a children's book. It combined text with photographs and told the story of a boy's first roundup. Young Hank wears blue jeans and a black hat in the book, rides a white horse, tags along with real cowboys, stares down a herd of cattle in a corral. You can see in these pictures why Hank was chosen for the part. His face is lively and expressive; he can ride; he can lasso; and he looks game, willing to jump a fence or chase after a steer ten times his size. The boy in the story starts out afraid of animals on the ranch, but in the end conquers his fear of cattle, snakes, and coyotes. There's a happy ending, and the final image echoes the last scene of a classic Hollywood Western, affirming the spirit of freedom and independence. Accompanied by an older cowhand and surrounded by a herd of cattle, young Hank rides his white horse across a vast, wide-open prairie, heading toward the horizon.

In life he did not get that sort of ending. He was buried at his ranch, in a simple wooden coffin made by friends.

The Most Dangerous Job

One night I visit a slaughterhouse somewhere in the High Plains. The slaughterhouse is one of the nation's largest. About five thousand head of cattle enter it every day, single file, and leave in a different form. Someone who has access to the plant, who's upset by its working conditions, offers to give me a tour. The slaughterhouse is an immense building, gray and square, about three stories high, with no windows on the front and no architectural clues to what's happening inside. My friend gives me a chain-mail apron and gloves, suggesting I try them on. Workers on the line wear about eight pounds of chain mail beneath their white coats, shiny steel armor that covers their hands, wrists, stomach, and back. The chain mail's designed to protect workers from cutting themselves and from being cut by other workers. But knives somehow manage to get past it. My host hands me some Wellingtons, the kind of knee-high rubber boots that English gentlemen wear in the countryside. 'Tuck your pants into the boots,' he says. 'We'll be walking through some blood.'

I put on a hardhat and climb a stairway. The sounds get louder, factory sounds, the noise of power tools and machinery, bursts of compressed air. We start at the end of the line, the fabricating room. Workers call it 'fab.' When we step inside, fab seems familiar: steel catwalks, pipes along the walls, a vast room, a maze of conveyer belts. This could be the Lamb Weston plant in Idaho, except hunks of red meat ride the belts instead of french fries. Some machines assemble cardboard boxes, others vacuum-seal subprimals of beef in clear plastic. The workers look extremely busy, but there's nothing unsettling about this part of the plant. You see meat like this all the time in the back of your local supermarket.

The fab room is cooled to about 40 degrees, and as you head up the line, the feel of the place starts to change. The pieces of meat get bigger. Workers – about half of them women, almost all of them young and Latino – slice meat with long slender knives. They stand at a table that's chest high, grab meat off a conveyer belt, trim away fat, throw meat back on the belt, toss the scraps onto a conveyer belt above them, and then grab more meat, all in a matter of seconds. I'm now struck by how many workers there are, hundreds of them, pressed close together, constantly moving, slicing. You see hardhats, white coats, flashes of steel. Nobody is smiling or chatting, they're too busy, anxiously trying not to fall behind. An old man walks past me, pushing a blue plastic barrel filled with scraps. A few workers carve the meat with Whizzards, small electric knives that have spinning round blades. The Whizzards look like the Norelco razors that Santa rides in the TV ads. I notice that a few of the women near me are sweating, even though the place is freezing cold.

Sides of beef suspended from an overhead trolley swing toward a group of men. Each worker has a large knife in one hand and a steel hook in the other. They grab the meat with their hooks and attack it fiercely with their knives. As they hack away, using all their strength, grunting, the place suddenly feels different, primordial. The machinery seems beside the point, and what's going on before me has been going on for thousands of years – the meat, the hook, the knife, men straining to cut more meat.

On the kill floor, what I see no longer unfolds in a logical manner. It's one strange image after another. A worker with a power saw slices cattle into halves as though they were two-by-fours, and then the halves swing by me into the cooler. It feels like a slaughterhouse now. Dozens of cattle, stripped of their skins, dangle on chains from their hind legs. My host stops and asks how I feel, if I want to go any further. This is where some people get sick. I feel fine, determined to see the whole process, the world that's been deliberately hidden. The kill floor is hot and humid. It stinks of manure. Cattle have a body temperature of about 101 degrees, and there are a lot of them in the room. Carcasses swing so fast along the rail that you have to keep an eye on them constantly, dodge them, watch your step, or one will slam you and throw you onto the bloody concrete floor. It happens to workers all the time.

I see: a man reach inside cattle and pull out their kidneys with his bare hands, then drop the kidneys down a metal chute, over and over again, as each animal passes by him; a stainless steel rack of tongues; Whizzards peeling meat off decapitated heads, picking them almost as clean as the white skulls painted by Georgia O'Keeffe. We wade through blood that's ankle deep and that pours down drains into huge vats below us. As we approach the start of the line, for the first time I hear the steady *pop, pop, pop* of live animals being stunned.

Now the cattle suspended above me look just like the cattle I've seen on ranches for years, but these ones are upside down swinging on hooks. For a moment, the sight seems unreal; there are so many of them, a herd of them, lifeless. And then I see a few hind legs still kicking, a final reflex action, and the reality comes hard and clear.

For eight and a half hours, a worker called a 'sticker' does nothing but stand in a river of blood, being drenched in blood, slitting the neck of a steer every ten seconds or so, severing its carotid artery. He uses a long knife and must hit exactly the right spot to kill the animal humanely. He hits that spot again and again. We walk up a slippery metal stairway and reach a small platform, where the production line begins. A man turns and smiles at me. He wears safety goggles and a hardhat. His face is splattered with gray matter and blood. He is the 'knocker,' the man who welcomes cattle to the building. Cattle walk down a narrow chute and pause in front of him, blocked by a gate, and then he shoots them in the head with a captive bolt stunner – a compressed-air gun attached to the ceiling by a long hose – which fires a steel bolt that knocks the cattle unconscious. The animals keep strolling up, oblivious to what comes next, and he stands over them and shoots. For eight and a half hours, he just shoots. As I stand there, he misses a few times and shoots the same animal twice. As soon as the steer falls, a worker grabs one of its hind legs, shackles it to a chain, and the chain lifts the huge animal into the air.

I watch the knocker knock cattle for a couple of minutes. The animals are powerful and imposing one moment and then gone in an instant, suspended from a rail, ready for carving. A steer slips from its chain, falls to the ground, and gets its head caught in one end of a conveyer belt. The production line stops as workers struggle to free the steer, stunned but alive, from the machinery. I've seen enough.

I step out of the building into the cool night air and follow the path that leads cattle into the slaughterhouse. They pass me, driven toward the building by workers with long white sticks that seem to glow in the dark. One steer, perhaps sensing instinctively what the other don't, turns and tries to run. But workers drive him back to join the rest. The cattle lazily walk single-file toward the muffled sounds, *pop, pop, pop*, coming from the open door.

The path has hairpin turns that prevent cattle from seeing what's in store and keep them relaxed. As the ramp gently slopes upward, the animals may think they're headed for another truck, another road trip – and they are, in unexpected ways. The ramp widens as it reaches ground level and then leads to a large cattle pen with wooden fences, a corral that belongs in a meadow, not here. As I walk along the fence, a group of cattle approach me, looking me straight in the eye, like dogs hoping for a treat, and follow me out of some mysterious impulse. I stop and try to absorb the whole scene: the cool breeze, the cattle and their gentle lowing, a cloudless sky, steam rising from the plant in the moonlight. And then I notice that the building does have one window, a small square of light on the second floor. It offers a glimpse of what's hidden behind this huge blank façade. Through the little window you can see bright red carcasses on hooks, going round and round.

Sharp Knives

Knocker, Sticker, Shackler, Rumper, First Legger, Knuckle Dropper, Navel Boner, Splitter Top/Bottom Butt, Feed Kill Chain – the names of job assignments at a modern slaughterhouse convey some of the brutality inherent in the work. Meatpacking is now the most dangerous job in the United States. The injury rate in a slaughterhouse is about three times higher than the rate in a typical American factory. Every year about one out of three meatpacking workers in this country – roughly forty-three thousand men and women – suffer an injury or a work-related illness that requires medical attention beyond first aid. There is strong evidence that these numbers, compiled by the Bureau of Labor Statistics, understate the number of meatpacking injuries that occur. Thousands of additional injuries and illnesses most likely go unrecorded.

Despite the use of conveyer belts, forklifts, dehiding machines, and a variety of power tools, most of the work in the nation's slaughterhouses is still performed by hand. Poultry plants can be largely mechanized, thanks to the breeding of chickens that are uniform in size. The birds in some Tyson factories are killed, plucked, gutted, beheaded, and sliced into cutlets by robots and machines. But cattle still come in all sizes and shapes, varying in weight by hundreds of pounds. The lack of a standardized steer has hindered the mechanization of beef plants. In one crucial respect meatpacking work has changed little in the past hundred years. At the dawn of the twenty-first century, amid an era of extraordinary technological advance, the most important tool in a modern slaughterhouse is a sharp knife.

Lacerations are the most common injuries suffered by meatpackers, who often stab themselves or stab someone working nearby. Tendinitis and cumulative trauma disorders are also quite common. Meatpacking workers routinely develop back problems, shoulder problems, carpal tunnel syndrome, and 'trigger finger' (a syndrome in which a finger becomes frozen in a curled position). Indeed, the rate of these cumulative trauma injuries in the meatpacking industry is far higher than the rate in any other American industry. It is almost thirty-five times higher than the national average in industry. Many slaughterhouse workers make a knife cut every two or three seconds, which adds up to about 10,000 cuts during an eight-hour shift. If the knife has become dull, additional pressure is placed on the worker's tendons, joints, and nerves. A dull knife can cause pain to extend from the cutting hand all the way down the spine.

Workers often bring their knives home and spend at least forty minutes a day keeping the edges smooth, sharp, and sanded, with no pits. One IBP worker, a small Guatemalan woman with graying hair, spoke with me in the cramped kitchen of her mobile home. As a pot of beans cooked on the stove, she sat in a wooden chair, gently rocking, telling the story of her life, of her journey north in search of work, the whole time sharpening big knives in her lap as though she were knitting a sweater.

The 'IBP revolution' has been directly responsible for many of the hazards that meatpacking workers now face. One of the leading determinants of the injury rate at a slaughterhouse today is the speed of the disassembly line. The faster it runs, the more likely that workers will get hurt. The old meatpacking plants in Chicago slaughtered about 50 cattle an hour. Twenty years ago, new plants in the High Plains slaughtered about 175 cattle an hour. Today some plants slaughter up to 400 cattle an hour – about half a dozen animals every minute, sent down a single production line, carved by workers desperate not to fall behind. While trying to keep up with the flow of meat, workers often neglect to resharpen their knives and thereby place more stress on their bodies. As the pace increases, so does the risk of accidental cuts and stabbings. 'I could always tell the line speed,' a former Monfort nurse told me, 'by the number of people with lacerations coming into my office.' People usually cut themselves; nevertheless, everyone on the line tries to stay alert. Meatpackers often work within inches of each other, wielding large knives. A simple mistake can cause a serious injury. A former IBP worker told me about boning knives suddenly flying out of hands and ricocheting off of machinery. 'They're very flexible,' she said, 'and they'll spring on you . . . zwing, and they're gone.'

Much like french fry factories, beef slaughterhouses often operate at profit margins as low as a few pennies a pound. The three meatpacking giants – ConAgra, IBP, and Excel – try to increase their earnings by maximizing the volume of production at each plant. Once a slaughterhouse is up and running, fully staffed, the profits it will earn are directly related to the speed of the line. A faster pace means higher profits. Market pressures now exert a perverse influence on the management of beef plants: the same factors that make these slaughterhouses relatively inefficient (the lack of mechanization, the reliance on human labor) encourage companies to make them even more dangerous (by speeding up the pace).

The unrelenting pressure of trying to keep up with the line has encouraged widespread methamphetamine use among meatpackers. Workers taking 'crank' feel charged and self-confident, ready for anything. Supervisors have been known to sell crank to their workers or to supply it free in return for certain favors, such as working a second shift. Workers who use methamphetamine may feel energized and invincible, but are actually putting themselves at much greater risk of having an accident. For obvious reasons, a modern slaughterhouse is not a safe place to be high.

In the days when labor unions were strong, workers could complain about excessive line speeds and injury rates without fear of getting fired. Today only one-third of IBP's workers belong to a union. Most of the nonunion workers are recent immigrants; many are illegals; and they are generally employed 'at will.' That means they can be fired without warning, for just about any reason. Such an arrangement does not encourage them to lodge complaints. Workers who have traveled a great distance for this job, who have families to support, who are earning ten times more an hour in a meatpacking plant than they could possibly earn back home, are wary about speaking out and losing everything. The line speeds and labor costs at IBP's nonunion plants now set the standard for the rest of the industry. Every other company must try to produce beef as quickly and cheaply as IBP does; slowing the pace to protect workers can lead to a competitive disadvantage.

Again and again workers told me that they are under tremendous pressure not to report injuries. The annual bonuses of plant foremen and supervisors are often based in part on the injury rate of their workers. Instead of creating a safer workplace, these bonus schemes encourage slaughterhouse managers to make sure that accidents and injuries go unreported. Missing fingers, broken bones, deep lacerations, and amputated limbs are difficult to conceal from authorities. But the dramatic and catastrophic injuries in a slaughterhouse are greatly outnumbered by less visible, though no less debilitating, ailments: torn muscles, slipped disks, pinched nerves.

If a worker agrees not to report an injury, a supervisor will usually shift him or her to an easier job for a while, providing some time to heal. If the injury seems more serious, a Mexican worker is often given the opportunity to return home for a while, to recuperate there, then come back to his or her slaughterhouse job in the United States. Workers who abide by these unwritten rules are treated respectfully; those who disobey are likely to be punished and made an example. As one former IBP worker explained, 'They're trying to deter you, period, from going to the doctor.'

From a purely economic point of view, injured workers are a drag on profits. They are less productive. Getting rid of them makes a good deal of financial sense, especially when new workers are readily available and inexpensive to train. Injured workers are often given some of the most unpleasant tasks in the slaughterhouse. Their hourly wages are cut. And through a wide variety of unsubtle means they are encouraged to quit.

Not all supervisors in a slaughterhouse behave like Simon Legree, shouting at workers, cursing them, belittling their injuries, always pushing them to move faster. But enough supervisors act that way to warrant the comparison. Production supervisors tend to be men in their late twenties and early thirties. Most are Anglos and don't speak Spanish, although more and more Latinos are being promoted to the job. They earn about $30,000 a year, plus bonuses and benefits. In many rural communities, being a supervisor at a meatpacking plant is one of the best jobs in town. It comes with a fair amount of pressure: a supervisor must meet production goals, keep the number of recorded injuries low, and most importantly, keep the meat flowing down the line without interruption. The job also brings enormous power. Each supervisor is like a little dictator in his or her section of the plant, largely free to boss, fire, berate, or reassign workers. That sort of power can lead to all sorts of abuses, especially when the hourly workers being supervised are women.

Many women told me stories about being fondled and grabbed on the production line, and the behavior of supervisors sets the tone for the other male workers. In February of 1999, a federal jury in Des Moines awarded $2.4 million to a female employee at an IBP slaughterhouse. According to the woman's testimony, coworkers had 'screamed obscenities and rubbed their bodies against hers while supervisors laughed.' Seven months later, Monfort agreed to settle a lawsuit filed by the U.S. Equal Employment Opportunity Commission on behalf of fourteen female workers in Texas. As part of the settlement, the company paid the women $900,000 and vowed to establish formal procedures for handling sexual harassment complaints. In their law-suit the women alleged that supervisors at a Monfort plant in Cactus, Texas, pressured them for dates and sex, and that male coworkers groped them, kissed them, and used animal parts in a sexually explicit manner.

The sexual relationships between supervisors and 'hourlies' are for the most part consensual. Many female workers optimistically regard sex with their supervisor as a way to gain a secure place in American society, a green card, a husband – or at the very least a transfer to an easier job at the plant. Some supervisors become meatpacking Casanovas, engaging in multiple affairs. Sex, drugs, and slaughterhouses may seem an unlikely combination, but as one former Monfort employee told me: 'Inside those walls is a different world that obeys different laws.' Late on the second shift, when it's dark outside, assignations take place in locker rooms, staff rooms, and parked cars, even on the catwalk over the kill floor.

The Worst

Some of the most dangerous jobs in meatpacking today are performed by the late-night cleaning crews. A large proportion of these workers are illegal immigrants. They are considered 'independent contractors,' employed not by the meatpacking firms but by sanitation companies. They earn hourly wages that are about one-third lower than those of regular production employees. And their work is so hard and so horrendous that words seem inadequate to describe it. The men and women who now clean the nation's slaughterhouses may arguably have the worst job in the United States. 'It takes a really dedicated person,' a former member of a cleaning crew told me, 'or a really desperate person to get the job done.'

When a sanitation crew arrives at a meatpacking plant, usually around midnight, it faces a mess of monumental proportions. Three to four thousand cattle, each weighing about a thousand pounds, have been slaughtered there that day. The place has to be clean by sunrise. Some of the workers wear water-resistant clothing; most don't. Their principal cleaning tool is a high-pressure hose that shoots a mixture of water and chlorine heated to about 180 degrees. As the water is sprayed, the plant fills with a thick, heavy fog. Visibility drops to as little as five feet. The conveyer belts and machinery are running. Workers stand on the belts, spraying them, riding them like moving sidewalks, as high as fifteen feet off the ground. Workers climb ladders with hoses and spray the catwalks. They get under tables and conveyer belts, climbing right into the bloody muck, cleaning out grease, fat, manure, leftover scraps of meat.

Glasses and safety goggles fog up. The inside of the plant heats up; temperatures soon exceed 100 degrees. 'It's hot, and it's foggy, and you can't see anything,' a former sanitation worker said. The crew members can't see or hear each other when the machinery's running. They routinely spray each other with burning hot, chemical-laden water. They are sickened by the fumes. Jesus, a soft-spoken employee of DCS Sanitation Management, Inc., the company that IBP uses in many of its plants, told me that every night on the job he gets terrible headaches. 'You feel it in your head,' he said. 'You feel it in your stomach, like you want to throw up.' A friend of his vomits whenever they clean the rendering area. Other workers tease the young man as he retches. Jesus says the stench in rendering is so powerful that it won't wash off; no matter how much soap you use after a shift, the smell comes home with you, seeps from your pores.

One night while Jesus was cleaning, a coworker forgot to turn off a machine, lost two fingers, and went into shock. An ambulance came and took him away, as everyone else continued to clean. He was back at work the following week. 'If one hand is no good,' the supervisor told him, 'use the other.' Another sanitation worker lost an arm in a machine. Now he folds towels in the locker room. The scariest job, according to Jesus, is cleaning the vents on the roof of the slaughterhouse. The vents become clogged with grease and dried blood. In the winter, when everything gets icy and the winds pick up, Jesus worries that a sudden gust will blow him off the roof into the darkness.

Although official statistics are not kept, the death rate among slaughterhouse sanitation crews is extraordinarily high. They are the ultimate in disposable workers: illegal, illiterate, impoverished, untrained. The nation's worst job can end in just about the worst way. Sometimes these workers are literally ground up and reduced to nothing.

A brief description of some cleaning-crew accidents over the past decade says more about the work and the danger than any set of statistics. At the Monfort plant in Grand Island, Nebraska, Richard Skala was beheaded by a dehiding machine. Carlos Vincente – an employee of T and G Service Company, a twenty-eight-year-old Guatemalan who'd been in the United States for only a week – was pulled into the cogs of a conveyer belt at an Excel plant in Fort Morgan, Colorado, and torn apart. Lorenzo Marin, Sr., an employee of DCS Sanitation, fell from the top of a skinning machine while cleaning it with a high-pressure hose, struck his head on the concrete floor of an IBP plant in Columbus Junction,

Iowa, and died. Another employee of DCS Sanitation, Salvador Hernandez-Gonzalez, had his head crushed by a pork-loin processing machine at an IBP plant in Madison, Nebraska. The same machine had fatally crushed the head of another worker, Ben Barone, a few years earlier. At a National Beef plant in Liberal, Kansas, Homer Stull climbed into a blood-collection tank to clean it, a filthy tank thirty feet high. Stull was overcome by hydrogen sulfide fumes. Two coworkers climbed into the tank and tried to rescue him. All three men died. Eight years earlier, Henry Wolf had been overcome by hydrogen sulfide fumes while cleaning the very same tank; Gary Sanders had tried to rescue him; both men died; and the Occupational Safety and Health Administration (OSHA) later fined National Beef for its negligence. The fine was $480 for each man's death.

Don't Get Caught

During the same years when the working conditions at America's meatpacking plants became more dangerous – when line speeds increased and illegal immigrants replaced skilled workers – the federal government greatly reduced the enforcement of health and safety laws. OSHA had long been despised by the nation's manufacturers, who considered the agency a source of meddlesome regulations and unnecessary red tape. When Ronald Reagan was elected president in 1980, OSHA was already underfunded and understaffed: its 1,300 inspectors were responsible for the safety of more than 5 million workplaces across the country. A typical American employer could expect an OSHA inspection about once every eighty years. Nevertheless, the Reagan administration was determined to reduce OSHA's authority even further, as part of the push for deregulation. The number of OSHA inspectors was eventually cut by 20 percent, and in 1981 the agency adopted a new policy of 'voluntary compliance.' Instead of arriving unannounced at a factory and performing an inspection, OSHA employees were required to look at a company's injury log before setting foot inside the plant. If the records showed an injury rate at the factory lower than the national average for all manufacturers, the OSHA inspector had to turn around and leave at once – without entering the plant, examining its equipment, or talking to any of its workers. These injury logs were kept and maintained by company officials.

For most of the 1980s OSHA's relationship with the meatpacking industry was far from adversarial. While the number of serious injuries rose, the number of OSHA inspections fell. The death of a worker on the job was punished with a fine of just a few hundred dollars. At a gathering of meat company executives in October of 1987, OSHA's safety director, Barry White, promised to change federal safety standards that 'appear amazingly stupid to you or overburdening or just not useful.' According to an account of the meeting later published in the *Chicago Tribune*, the safety director at OSHA – the federal official most responsible for protecting the lives of meatpacking workers – acknowledged his own lack of qualification for the job. 'I know very well that you know more about safety and health in the meat industry than I do,' White told the executives. 'And you know more about safety and health in the meat industry than any single employee at OSHA.'

OSHA's voluntary compliance policy did indeed reduce the number of recorded injuries in meatpacking plants. It did not, however, reduce the number of people getting hurt. It merely encouraged companies, in the words of a subsequent congressional investigation, 'to understate injuries, to falsify records, and to cover up accidents.' At the IBP beef plant in Dakota City, Nebraska, for example, the company kept two sets of injury logs: one of them recording every injury and illness at the slaughterhouse, the other provided to visiting OSHA inspectors and researchers from the Bureau of Labor Statistics. During a three-month period in 1985, the first log recorded 1,800 injuries and illnesses at the plant. The OSHA log recorded only 160 – a discrepancy of more than 1,000 percent.

At congressional hearings on meatpacking in 1987, Robert L. Peterson, the chief executive of IBP, denied under oath that two sets of logs were ever kept and called IBP's safety record 'the best of the best.' Congressional investigators later got hold of both logs – and found that the injury rate at its Dakota City plant was as much as one-third higher than the average rate in the meatpacking industry. Congressional investigators also discovered that IBP had altered injury records at its beef plant in Emporia, Kansas. Another leading meatpacking company, John Morrell, was caught lying about injuries at its plant in Sioux Falls, South Dakota. The

congressional investigation concluded that these companies had failed to report 'serious injuries such as frac-
tures, concussions, major cuts, hernias, some requiring
hospitalization, surgery, even amputation.'

Congressman Tom Lantos, whose subcommittee
conducted the meatpacking inquiry, called IBP 'one of
the most irresponsible and reckless corporations in
America.' A Labor Department official called the
company's behavior 'the worst example of under-
reporting injuries and illnesses to workers ever encoun-
tered in OSHA's sixteen-year history.' Nevertheless,
Robert L. Peterson was never charged with perjury for
his misleading testimony before Congress. Investigators
argued that it would be difficult to prove 'conclusively'
that Peterson had 'willfully' lied. In 1987 IBP was fined
$2.6 million by OSHA for underreporting injuries and
later fined an additional $3.1 million for the high rate of
cumulative trauma injuries at the Dakota City plant.
After the company introduced a new safety program
there, the fines were reduced to $975,000 – a sum that
might have appeared large at the time, yet represented
about one one-hundredth of a percent of IBP's annual
revenues.

Three years after the OSHA fines, a worker named
Kevin Wilson injured his back at an IBP slaughterhouse
in Council Bluffs, Iowa. Wilson went to see Diane Arndt,
a nurse at the plant, who sent him to a doctor selected
by the company. Wilson's injury was not serious, the
doctor said, later assigning him to light duty at the plant.
Wilson sought a second opinion; the new doctor said
that he had a disk injury that required a period of

absence from work. When Wilson stopped reporting for light duty, IBP's corporate security department began to conduct surveillance of his house. Eleven days after Wilson's new doctor told IBP that back surgery might be required, Diane Arndt called the doctor and said that IBP had obtained a videotape of Wilson engaging in strenuous physical activities at home. The doctor felt deceived, met with Wilson, accused him of being a liar, refused to provide him with any more treatment, and told him to get back to work. Convinced that no such videotape existed and that IBP had fabricated the entire story in order to deny him medical treatment, Kevin Wilson sued the company for slander.

The lawsuit eventually reached the Iowa Supreme Court. In a decision that received little media attention, the Supreme Court upheld a lower court's award of $2 million to Wilson and described some of IBP's unethical practices. The court found that seriously injured workers were required to show up at the IBP plant briefly each day so that the company could avoid reporting 'lost workdays' to OSHA. Some workers were compelled to show up for work on the same day as a surgery or the day after an amputation. 'IBP's management was aware of, and participated in, this practice,' the Iowa Supreme Court noted. IBP nurses regularly entered false information into the plant's computer system, reclassifying injuries so that they didn't have to be reported to OSHA. Injured workers who proved uncooperative were assigned to jobs 'watching gauges in the rendering plant, where they were subjected to an atrocious smell while hog remains were boiled down into fertilizers and blood was drained into tanks.' According to evidence introduced in court, Diane Arndt had a low opinion of the workers whose injuries she was supposed to be treating. The IBP nurse called them 'idiots' and 'jerks,' telling doctors that 'this guy's a crybaby' and 'this guy's full of shit.' She later admitted that Wilson's back injury was legitimate. The Iowa Supreme Court concluded that the lies she told in this medical case, as well as in others, had been partly motivated by IBP's financial incentive program, which gave staff members bonuses and prizes when the number of lost workdays was kept low. The program, in the court's opinion, was 'somewhat disingenuously called "the safety award system."'

IBP's attitude toward worker safety was hardly unique in the industry, according to Edward Murphy's testimony before Congress in 1992. Murphy had served as the safety director of the Monfort beef plant in Grand Island. After two workers were killed there in 1991, Monfort fired him. Murphy claimed that he had battled the company for years over safety issues and that Monfort had unfairly made him the scapegoat for its own illegal behavior. The company later paid him an undisclosed sum of money to settle a civil lawsuit over wrongful termination.

Murphy told Congress that during his tenure at the Grand Island plant, Monfort maintained two sets of injury logs, routinely lied to OSHA, and shredded documents requested by OSHA. He wanted Congress to know that the safety lapses at the plant were not accidental. They stemmed directly from Monfort's corporate philosophy, which Murphy described in these terms: 'The first commandment is that only production counts . . . The employee's duty is to follow orders. Period. As I was repeatedly told, "Do what I tell you, even if it is illegal . . . Don't get caught."'

A lawsuit filed in May of 1998 suggests that little has changed since IBP was caught keeping two sets of injury logs more than a decade ago. Michael D. Ferrell, a former vice president at IBP, contends that the real blame for the high injury rate at the company lies not with the workers, supervisors, nurses, safety directors, or plant managers, but with IBP's top executives. Ferrell had ample opportunity to observe their decision-making process. Among other duties, he was in charge of the health and safety programs at IBP.

When Ferrell accepted the job in 1991, after many years as an industrial engineer at other firms, he believed that IBP's desire to improve worker safety was sincere. According to his legal complaint, Ferrell later discovered that IBP's safety records were routinely falsified and that the company cared more about production than anything else. Ferrell was fired by IBP in 1997, not long after a series of safety problems at a slaughterhouse in Palestine, Texas. The circumstances surrounding his firing are at the heart of the lawsuit. On December 4, 1996, an OSHA inspection of the Palestine plant found a number of serious violations and imposed a fine of $35,125. Less than a week later, a worker named Clarence Dupree lost an arm in a bone-crushing machine. And two days after that, another worker, Willie Morris, was killed by an ammonia gas explosion. Morris's body lay on the floor for hours, just ten feet from the door, as toxic gas filled the building. Nobody at the plant had been trained to use hazardous-materials gas masks or protective suits; the equipment sat in a locked storage room. Ferrell flew to Texas and toured the plant after the accidents. He thought the facility was in terrible shape – with a cooling system that violated OSHA standards, faulty wiring that threatened to cause a mass electrocution, and safety mechanisms that had deliberately been disabled with magnets. He wanted the slaughterhouse to be shut down immediately, and it was. Two months later, Ferrell lost his job.

In his lawsuit seeking payment for wrongful termination, Ferrell contends that he was fired for giving the order to close the Palestine plant. He claims that IBP had never before shut down a slaughterhouse purely for safety reasons and that Robert L. Peterson was enraged by the decision. IBP disputes this version of events, contending that Ferrell had never fit into IBP's corporate culture, that he delegated too much authority, and that he had not, in fact, made the decision to shut down the Palestine plant. According to IBP, the decision to shut it was made after a unanimous vote by its top executives.

IBP's Palestine slaughterhouse reopened in January of 1997. It was shut down again a year later – this time by the USDA. Federal inspectors cited the plant for 'inhumane slaughter' and halted production there for one week, an extremely rare penalty imposed for the mistreatment of cattle. In 1999 IBP closed the plant. As of this writing, it sits empty, awaiting a buyer.

The Value of an Arm

When I first visited Greeley in 1997, Javier Ramirez was president of the UFCW, Local 990, the union representing employees at the Monfort beef plant. The National Labor Relations Board had ruled that Monfort committed 'numerous, pervasive, and outrageous' violations of labor law after reopening the Greeley beef plant in 1982, discriminating against former union members at hiring time and intimidating new workers during a union election. Former employees who'd been treated unfairly ultimately received a $10.6 million settlement. After a long and arduous organizing drive, workers at the Monfort beef plant voted to join the UFCW in 1992. Javier Ramirez is thirty-one and knows a fair amount about beef. His father is Ruben Ramirez, the Chicago union leader. Javier grew up around slaughterhouses and watched the meatpacking industry abandon his hometown for the High Plains. Instead of finding another line of work, he followed the industry to Colorado, trying to gain better wages and working conditions for the mainly Latino workforce.

The UFCW has given workers in Greeley the ability to challenge unfair dismissals, file grievances against supervisors, and report safety lapses without fear of reprisal. But the union's power is limited by the plant's high turnover rate. Every year a new set of workers must be persuaded to support the UFCW. The plant's revolving door is not conducive to worker solidarity. At the moment some of the most pressing issues for the UFCW are related to the high injury rate at the slaughterhouse. It is a constant struggle not only to prevent workers from getting hurt, but also to gain them proper medical treatment and benefits once they've been hurt.

Colorado was one of the first states to pass a workers' compensation law. The idea behind the legislation, enacted in 1919, was to provide speedy medical care and a steady income to workers injured on the job. Workers' comp was meant to function much like no-fault insurance. In return for surrendering the right to sue employers for injuries, workers were supposed to receive immediate benefits. Similar workers' comp plans were adopted throughout the United States. In 1991, Colorado started another trend, becoming one of the first states to impose harsh restrictions on workers' comp payments. In addition to reducing the benefits afforded to injured employees, Colorado's new law granted employers the right to choose the physician who'd determine the severity of any work-related ailment. Enormous power over workers' comp claims was handed to company doctors.

Many other states subsequently followed Colorado's lead and cut back their workers' comp benefits. The Colorado bill, promoted as 'workers' comp reform,' was first introduced in the legislature by Tom Norton, the president of the Colorado State Senate and a conservative Republican. Norton represented Greeley, where his wife, Kay, was the vice president of legal and governmental affairs at ConAgra Red Meat.

In most businesses, a high injury rate would prompt insurance companies to demand changes in the workplace. But ConAgra, IBP, and the other large meat-

packing firms are self-insured. They are under no
pressure from independent underwriters and have a
strong incentive to keep workers' comp payments to a
bare minimum. Every penny spent on workers' comp
is one less penny of corporate revenue.

Javier Ramirez began to educate Monfort workers
about their legal right to get workers' comp benefits after
an injury at the plant. Many workers don't realize that
such insurance even exists. The workers' comp claim
forms look intimidating, especially to people who don't
speak any English and can't read any language. Filing a
claim, challenging a powerful meatpacking company, and
placing faith in the American legal system requires a good
deal of courage, especially for a recent immigrant.

When a workers' comp claim involves an injury that
is nearly impossible to refute (such as an on-the-job
amputation), the meatpacking companies generally
agree to pay. But when injuries are less visible (such as
those stemming from cumulative trauma) the meatpackers often prolong the whole workers' comp process
through litigation, insisting upon hearings and filing
seemingly endless appeals. Some of the most painful
and debilitating injuries are the hardest to prove.

Today it can take years for an injured worker to
receive workers' comp benefits. During that time, he or
she must pay medical bills and find a source of income.
Many rely on public assistance. The ability of meatpacking firms to delay payment discourages many
injured workers from ever filing workers' comp claims.
It leads others to accept a reduced sum of money as
part of a negotiated settlement in order to cover medical

bills. The system now leaves countless unskilled and uneducated manual workers poorly compensated for injuries that will forever hamper their ability to earn a living. The few who win in court and receive full benefits are hardly set for life. Under Colorado's new law, the payment for losing an arm is $36,000. An amputated finger gets you anywhere from $2,200 to $4,500, depending on which one is lost. And 'serious permanent disfigurement about the head, face, or parts of the body normally exposed to public view' entitles you to a maximum of $2,000.

As workers' comp benefits have become more difficult to obtain, the threat to workplace safety has grown more serious. During the first two years of the Clinton administration, OSHA seemed like a revitalized agency. It began to draw up the first ergonomics standards for the nation's manufacturers, aiming to reduce cumulative trauma disorders. The election of 1994, however, marked a turning point. The Republican majority in Congress that rose to power that year not only impeded the adoption of ergonomics standards but also raised questions about the future of OSHA. Working closely with the U.S. Chamber of Commerce and the National Association of Manufacturers, House Republicans have worked hard to limit OSHA's authority. Congressman Cass Ballenger, a Republican from North Carolina, introduced legislation that would require OSHA to spend at least half of its budget on 'consultation' with businesses, instead of enforcement. This new budget requirement would further reduce the number of OSHA inspections, which by the late 1990s had already reached an all-time low. Ballenger has long opposed OSHA inspections, despite the fact that near his own district a fire at a poultry plant killed twenty-five workers in 1991. The plant had never been inspected by OSHA, its emergency exits had been chained shut, and the bodies of workers were found in piles near the locked doors. Congressman Joel Hefley, a Colorado Republican whose district includes Colorado Springs, has introduced a bill that makes Ballenger's seem moderate. Hefley's 'OSHA Reform Act' would essentially repeal the Occupational Safety and Health Act of 1970. It would forbid OSHA from conducting any workplace inspections or imposing any fines.

Kenny

During my trips to meatpacking towns in the High Plains I met dozens of workers who'd been injured. Each of their stories was different, yet somehow familiar, linked by common elements – the same struggle to receive proper medical care, the same fear of speaking out, the same underlying corporate indifference. We are human beings, more than one person told me, but they treat us like animals. The workers I met wanted their stories to be told. They wanted people to know about what is happening right now. A young woman who'd injured her back and her right hand at the Greeley plant said to me. 'I want to get on top of a rooftop and scream my lungs out so that somebody will hear.' The voices and faces of these workers are indelibly with me, as is the sight of their hands, the light brown skin criss-crossed with white scars. Although I cannot tell all of their stories, a few need to be mentioned. Like all lives, they can be used as examples or serve as representative types. But ultimately they are unique, individual, impossible to define or replace – the opposite of how this system has treated them.

Raoul was born in Zapoteca, Mexico, and did construction work in Anaheim before moving to Colorado. He speaks no English. After hearing a Monfort ad on a Spanish-language radio station, he applied for a job at the Greeley plant. One day Raoul reached into a processing machine to remove a piece of meat. The machine accidentally went on. Raoul's arm got stuck, and it took workers twenty minutes to get it out. The machine had to be taken apart. An ambulance brought Raoul to the hospital, where a deep gash in his shoulder was sewn shut. A tendon had been severed. After getting stitches and a strong prescription painkiller, he was driven back to the slaughterhouse and put back on the production line. Bandaged, groggy, and in pain, one arm tied in a sling, Raoul spent the rest of the day wiping blood off cardboard boxes with his good hand.

Renaldo was another Monfort worker who spoke no English, an older man with graying hair. He developed carpal tunnel syndrome while cutting meat. The injury got so bad that sharp pain shot from his hand all the way up to his shoulder. At night it hurt so much he could not fall asleep in bed. Instead he would fall asleep sitting in a chair beside the bed where his wife lay. For three years he slept in that chair every night.

Kenny Dobbins was a Monfort employee for almost sixteen years. He was born in Keokuk, Iowa, had a tough childhood and an abusive stepfather, left home at the age of thirteen, went in and out of various schools, never learned to read, did various odd jobs, and wound up at the Monfort slaughterhouse in Grand Island, Nebraska. He started working there in 1979, right after the company bought it from Swift. He was twenty-three. He worked in the shipping department at first, hauling boxes that weighed as much as 120 pounds. Kenny could handle it, though. He was a big man, muscular and six-foot-five, and nothing in his life had ever been easy.

One day Kenny heard someone yell, 'Watch out!' then turned around and saw a ninety-pound box falling from an upper level of the shipping department. Kenny caught the box with one arm, but the momentum threw him against a conveyer belt, and the metal teeth on the rim of the belt pierced his lower back. The company doctor bandaged Kenny's back and said the pain was just a pulled muscle. Kenny never filed for workers' comp, stayed home for a few days, then returned to work. He had a wife and three children to support. For the next few months, he was in terrible pain. 'It hurt so fucking bad you wouldn't believe it,' he told me. He saw another doctor, got a second opinion. The new doctor said Kenny had a pair of severely herniated disks. Kenny had back surgery, spent a month in the hospital, got sent to a pain clinic when the operation didn't work. His marriage broke up amid the stress and financial difficulty. Fourteen months after the injury, Kenny returned to the slaughterhouse. 'GIVE UP AFTER BACK SURGERY? NOT

KEN DOBBINS!!' a Monfort newsletter proclaimed. 'Ken has learned how to handle the rigors of working in a packing plant and is trying to help others do the same. Thanks, Ken, and keep up the good work.'

Kenny felt a strong loyalty to Monfort. He could not read, possessed few skills other than his strength, and the company had still given him a job. When Monfort decided to reopen its Greeley plant with a non-union workforce, Kenny volunteered to go there and help. He did not think highly of labor unions. His supervisors told him that unions had been responsible for shutting down meatpacking plants all over the country. When the UFCW tried to organize the Greeley slaughter-house, Kenny became an active and outspoken member of an anti-union group.

At the Grand Island facility, Kenny had been restricted to light duty after his injury. But his supervisor in Greeley said that old restrictions didn't apply in this new job. Soon Kenny was doing tough, physical labor once again, wielding a knife and grabbing forty- to fifty-pound pieces of beef off a table. When the pain became unbearable, he was transferred to ground beef, then to rendering. According to a former manager at the Greeley plant, Monfort was trying to get rid of Kenny, trying to make his work so unpleasant that he'd quit. Kenny didn't realize it. 'He still believes in his heart that people are honest and good,' the former manager said about Kenny. 'And he's wrong.'

As part of the job in rendering, Kenny sometimes had to climb into gigantic blood tanks and gut bins, reach to the bottom of them with his long arms, and unclog the drains. One day he was unexpectedly called to work over the weekend. There had been a problem with *Salmonella* contamination. The plant needed to be disinfected, and some of the maintenance workers had refused to do it. In his street clothes, Kenny began cleaning the place, climbing into tanks and spraying a liquid chlorine mix. Chlorine is a hazardous chemical that can be inhaled or absorbed through the skin, causing a litany of health problems. Workers who spray it need to wear protective gloves, safety goggles, a self-contained respirator, and full coveralls. Kenny's supervisor gave him a paper dust mask to wear, but it quickly dissolved. After eight hours of working with the chlorine in unventilated areas, Kenny went home and fell ill. He was rushed to the hospital and placed in an oxygen tent. His lungs had been burned by the chemicals. His body was covered in blisters. Kenny spent a month in the hospital.

Kenny eventually recovered from the overexposure to chlorine, but it left his chest feeling raw, made him susceptible to colds and sensitive to chemical aromas. He went back to work at the Greeley plant. He had remarried, didn't know what other kind of work to do, still felt loyal to the company. He was assigned to an early morning shift. He had to drive an old truck from one part of the slaughterhouse complex to another. The truck was filled with leftover scraps of meat. The headlights and the wipers didn't work. The windshield was filthy and cracked. One cold, dark morning in the middle of winter, Kenny became disoriented while driving. He stopped the truck, opened the door, got out to see where he was – and was struck by a train. It knocked his glasses off, threw him up in the air, and knocked both of his work boots off. The train was moving slowly, or he would've been killed. Kenny somehow made it back to the plant, barefoot and bleeding from deep gashes in his back and his face. He spent two weeks at the hospital, then went back to work.

One day, Kenny was in rendering and saw a worker about to stick his head into a pre-breaker machine, a device that uses hundreds of small hammers to pulverize gristle and bone into a fine powder. The worker had just turned the machine off, but Kenny knew the hammers inside were still spinning. It takes fifteen minutes for the machine to shut down completely. Kenny yelled, 'Stop!' but the worker didn't hear him. And so Kenny ran across the room, grabbed the man by the seat of his pants, and pulled him away from the machine an instant before it would have pulverized him. To honor this act of bravery, Monfort gave Kenny an award for 'Outstanding Achievement in CONCERN FOR FELLOW WORKERS.' The award was a paper certificate, signed by his supervisor and the plant safety manager.

Kenny later broke his leg stepping into a hole in the slaughterhouse's concrete floor. On another occasion he shattered an ankle, an injury that required surgery and the insertion of five steel pins. Now Kenny had to wear a metal brace on one leg in order to walk, an elaborate, spring-loaded brace that cost $2,000. Standing for long periods caused him great pain. He was given a job recycling old knives at the plant. Despite his many injuries, the job required him to climb up and down three flights of narrow stairs carrying garbage bags filled with knives.

In December of 1995 Kenny felt a sharp pain in his chest while lifting some boxes. He thought it was a heart attack. His union steward took him to see the nurse, who said it was just a pulled muscle and sent Kenny home. He was indeed having a massive heart attack. A friend rushed Kenny to a nearby hospital. A stent was inserted in his heart, and the doctors told Kenny that he was lucky to be alive.

Not long afterward, Monfort fired Kenny Dobbins. Despite the fact that Kenny had been with the company for almost sixteen years, despite the fact that he was first in seniority at the Greeley plant, that he'd cleaned blood tanks with his bare hands, fought the union, done whatever the company had asked him to do, suffered injuries that would've killed weaker men, nobody from Monfort called him with the news. Nobody even bothered to write him. Kenny learned that he'd been fired when his payments to the company health insurance plan kept being returned by the post office. He called Monfort repeatedly to find out what was going on, and a sympathetic clerk in the claims office finally told Kenny that the checks were being returned because he was no longer a Monfort employee. When I asked company spokesmen to comment on the accuracy of Kenny's story, they would neither confirm nor deny any of the details.

Today Kenny is in poor health. His heart is permanently damaged. His immune system seems shot. His back hurts, his ankle hurts, and every so often he coughs up blood. He is unable to work at any job. His wife, Clara – who's half-Latina and half-Cheyenne, and looks like a younger sister of Cher's – was working as a nursing home attendant when Kenny had the heart attack. Amid the stress of his illness, she developed a serious kidney ailment. She is unemployed and recuperating from a kidney transplant.

As I sat in the living room of their Greeley home, its walls decorated with paintings of wolves, Denver Broncos memorabilia, and an American flag, Kenny and Clara told me about their financial condition. After almost sixteen years on the job, Kenny did not get any pension from Monfort. The company challenged his workers' comp claim and finally agreed – three years after the initial filing – to pay him a settlement of $35,000. Fifteen percent of that money went to Kenny's lawyer, and the rest is long gone. Some months Kenny has to hock things to get money for Clara's medicine. They have two teenage children and live on Social Security payments. Kenny's health insurance, which costs more than $600 a month, is about to run out. His anger at Monfort, his feelings of betrayal, are of truly biblical proportions.

'They used me to the point where I had no body parts left to give,' Kenny said, struggling to maintain his composure. 'Then they just tossed me into the trash can.' Once strong and powerfully built, he now walks with difficulty, tires easily, and feels useless, as though his life were over. He is forty-five years old.

POCKET PENGUINS

1. Lady Chatterley's Trial
2. **Eric Schlosser** Cogs in the Great Machine
3. **Nick Hornby** Otherwise Pandemonium
4. **Albert Camus** Summer in Algiers
5. **P. D. James** Innocent House
6. **Richard Dawkins** The View from Mount Improbable
7. **India Knight** On Shopping
8. **Marian Keyes** Nothing Bad Ever Happens in Tiffany's
9. **Jorge Luis Borges** The Mirror of Ink
10. **Roald Dahl** A Taste of the Unexpected
11. **Jonathan Safran Foer** The Unabridged Pocketbook of Lightning
12. **Homer** The Cave of the Cyclops
13. **Paul Theroux** Two Stars
14. **Elizabeth David** Of Pageants and Picnics
15. **Anaïs Nin** Artists and Models
16. **Antony Beevor** Christmas at Stalingrad
17. **Gustave Flaubert** The Desert and the Dancing Girls
18. **Anne Frank** The Secret Annexe
19. **James Kelman** Where I Was
20. **Hari Kunzru** Noise
21. **Simon Schama** The Bastille Falls
22. **William Trevor** The Dressmaker's Child
23. **George Orwell** In Defence of English Cooking
24. **Michael Moore** Idiot Nation
25. **Helen Dunmore** Rose, 1944
26. **J. K. Galbraith** The Economics of Innocent Fraud
27. **Gervase Phinn** The School Inspector Calls
28. **W. G. Sebald** Young Austerlitz
29. **Redmond O'Hanlon** Borneo and the Poet
30. **Ali Smith** Ali Smith's Supersonic 70s
31. **Sigmund Freud** Forgetting Things
32. **Simon Armitage** King Arthur in the East Riding
33. **Hunter S. Thompson** Happy Birthday, Jack Nicholson
34. **Vladimir Nabokov** Cloud, Castle, Lake
35. **Niall Ferguson** 1914: Why the World Went to War

POCKET PENGUINS

36. **Muriel Spark** The Snobs
37. **Steven Pinker** Hotheads
38. **Tony Harrison** Under the Clock
39. **John Updike** Three Trips
40. **Will Self** Design Faults in the Volvo 760 Turbo
41. **H. G. Wells** The Country of the Blind
42. **Noam Chomsky** Doctrines and Visions
43. **Jamie Oliver** Something for the Weekend
44. **Virginia Woolf** Street Haunting
45. **Zadie Smith** Martha and Hanwell
46. **John Mortimer** The Scales of Justice
47. **F. Scott Fitzgerald** The Diamond as Big as the Ritz
48. **Roger McGough** The State of Poetry
49. **Ian Kershaw** Death in the Bunker
50. **Gabriel García Márquez** Seventeen Poisoned Englishmen
51. **Steven Runciman** The Assault on Jerusalem
52. **Sue Townsend** The Queen in Hell Close
53. **Primo Levi** Iron Potassium Nickel
54. **Alistair Cooke** Letters from Four Seasons
55. **William Boyd** Protobiography
56. **Robert Graves** Caligula
57. **Melissa Bank** The Worst Thing a Suburban Girl Could Imagine
58. **Truman Capote** My Side of the Matter
59. **David Lodge** Scenes of Academic Life
60. **Anton Chekhov** The Kiss
61. **Claire Tomalin** Young Bysshe
62. **David Cannadine** The Aristocratic Adventurer
63. **P. G. Wodehouse** Jeeves and the Impending Doom
64. **Franz Kafka** The Great Wall of China
65. **Dave Eggers** Short Short Stories
66. **Evelyn Waugh** The Coronation of Haile Selassie
67. **Pat Barker** War Talk
68. **Jonathan Coe** 9th & 13th
69. **John Steinbeck** Murder
70. **Alain de Botton** On Seeing and Noticing